*River swan*
Annan Photo Features

# THE Thames

## LONDON'S RIVER

RIVERS OF THE WORLD

# THE

# THAMES

# LONDON'S RIVER

## by NOEL STREATFEILD

*Illustrations by Kurt Wiese*
*Maps by Fred Kliem*

**GARRARD PUBLISHING COMPANY**
CHAMPAIGN, ILLINOIS

*A Thames River barge passes the Houses of Parliament in London.*

The British Travel Association

NANCY LARRICK, ED.D.,
IS THE EDUCATIONAL ADVISOR FOR THIS SERIES

*For reading the manuscript of this book and checking the accuracy of its content, the author and editor are grateful to Dr. H. E. Priestley, educator and historian, South Benfleet, Essex.*

Manufactured in the United States of America
Library of Congress Catalog Number 64-12628

The British Travel Association

# Contents

SCOTLAND

NORTH SEA

IRISH SEA

DUBLIN

ENGLAND

WALES

THE THAMES RIVER

THAMES    OXFORD    LONDON

READING

THAMES

SOUTHAMPTON

ENGLISH CHANNEL

FRANC

SCALE IN MILES

0    25    50    75    100    125    150

W    E

# 1. "The Brook"

The Thames (pronounced *Temz*) is a very old river. The British call it affectionately "Old Father Thames." It is 260 miles long. It starts its life as a mere trickle in the beautiful Cotswold Hills, in a part of England called Gloucestershire. Some rivers are exciting and violent with huge waterfalls and grand scenery. There is nothing violent or exciting about the Thames. It just flows along through quiet landscapes, joining other rivers and waterways to itself as it travels.

Because so many rivers and waterways join the Thames, it becomes a grand big river by the time it reaches London. While it is a country river learning to be a big river, the Thames flows slowly. It seems to move at a countryman's plodding speed. In fact it moves so gently it is difficult to believe it will ever grow up to be the important bustling river that London knows.

While the river is still very young it is called affectionately "The Brook." Here it belongs to the fishermen, who drowse away summer hours on its banks. It also belongs to all the water birds and animals who make their homes on the waterside, or find their food on it.

Some of the birds have lovely names—kingfishers, herons, sedge warblers, mallards, moorhens and coots. Nothing is prettier in the spring than to see a mother moorhen showing the river to her babies.

*Mrs. Mallard sails with Mr. Mallard near the riverbank.*

Annan Photo Features

*The tiny vole creeps in and out of the grasses.*

Annan Photo Features

The animals seem to have fun on the riverbanks. Water rats peer out with their bright little eyes. Otters play glorious rough-and-tumble games. Voles, snuffling along, go their secret ways.

Except in wintertime the riverbank is gay with flowers—celandines, primroses, kingcups, cowslips and violets in the spring; wild thyme, meadowsweet, viper's bugloss, harebells and rock roses in the summer. When the autumn comes,

9

*The otter hauls himself out of the backwater.*

sprays of travelers' joy spill down the riverbanks to trail on the water. Then, through the mist which rises from the river, red berries gleam from the hedges.

There is a lot of life in the river itself. The fish are small in "The Brook," mostly minnows and sticklebacks. Luckily, there are plenty of water weeds for little fish to live on. In the spring children run to the riverbank with jam jars to collect tadpoles. There are river insects,

10

too, which hatch out in the weeds: lovely dragon-flies, mayflies, water beetles and, skimming busily about, water boatmen.

The lords of the river are the swans, which play a part in almost every stage of the river's life. They sail majestically past the ordinary river dwellers, looking down their proud beaks at less important birds. "If we all had our rights, we

*The swans seem to own the river.*

should wear crowns," they seem to be saying.

The Thames is a very winding river. Sometimes it wanders so much that it loops back and passes itself. On one of these backward loops, it passes through a tiny village called Lechlade. Nobody could guess it now, but it was a big town in the Middle Ages. In those days some of the best wool in the country came from sheep bred near Lechlade in Gloucestershire.

Lechlade is important now for another reason, for here four little rivers join the Thames. Now, for the first time, the Thames is big enough to carry boats. They must be shallow boats, though, because the river is still small and not deep.

Beyond Lechlade the boats on the Thames must pass through a series of locks. These are necessary because from the source of the river to its mouth there is a drop of 376 feet. Locks are like giant stairsteps up or down the river. When a boat goes into a lock, it is confined in a small dock closed by sluice gates. Water then flows into the dock or out of it, according to whether the

*Water pours into the narrow channel, or lock, and lifts the boats to the next level of the canal.*

boat is traveling upriver or down. This shifts the boat from one level to another. As soon as the water in the dock is level with the water outside, the sluice gates are opened and the boat can go on its way.

One of the most interesting locks is Shifford Lock. At this place King Alfred the Great, more than 1,100 years ago, called a meeting of important men. This meeting was a very early beginning of Parliament, the group which makes the laws of Great Britain. The British have had a true Parliament for about 700 years.

British children do not remember Alfred the Great because of that meeting of notables. They know him as the king who burned the cakes. The story is that King Alfred fled from his enemies and took shelter in the cottage of a peasant woman. Because of his disguise she did not recognize him. When she went out, she asked the stranger to mind the cakes she was baking. On her return she found the cakes burned black. This made her so angry that she boxed the king's ears. Royal ears have seldom been boxed, which is why British children remember Alfred the Great as the king who burned the cakes.

*Alfred the Great had his ears boxed.*

*The towers
and spires
of Oxford.*

# 2.  Down from Oxford

The Thames, growing bigger and bigger as rivers flow into it, moves on its way to the university town of Oxford. The Thames does not flow through Oxford, but just outside the town it is joined by the river Cherwell. This makes the Thames large enough for boat races and regattas.

Oxford University is famous for its boating events. The best known are the bumping races, which last a week. The competing boats line up for the start in the order in which they finished the race the previous year. When the "Off" is

sounded, each team tries to row so fast that their bow bumps the stern of the boat ahead. Oxford also holds a regatta each summer.

Beyond Oxford so many rivers and waterways join the Thames that it soon becomes big enough for all kinds of boats—rowing boats, motor launches, canoes and, where the river is wide enough, sailing boats. Because the Thames has a gravelly bottom into which a pole will not sink, a favorite boat is a punt.

Sailing boats usually belong to clubs. This is because boys and girls come from miles away to sail them. So a clubhouse is needed in which the boats can be stored when they are not afloat.

Here the Thames is a pleasure river. People who love the river and boats live on its banks. At one time only rich people built river houses. A hundred years ago a river house was a great mansion in park-like grounds with fine trees. At the water's edge there was always a boathouse. But times have changed and today nobody wants big houses. In their places are little houses or

17

*Crews of eight row in the annual Oxford regatta.*

bungalows, sometimes just a house trailer. There are no boathouses now. Instead, the family boat is moored on the river in the summer, and stored at the back of the garage in the winter.

In olden days the mansion children in their silks and muslins were attended by servants. Or they were escorted to the boathouse by tutors and governesses. Today's children in shorts and jeans are unattended so they wear life jackets. But they all in their day shared one love. Like Water Rat in *The Wind in the Willows* they knew "there is *nothing*—absolutely nothing—half so much worth doing as simply messing about in boats."

As the Thames grows larger, it passes the town of Reading. Here it starts to carry pleasure steamers. These are far bigger boats than have been seen before, and can take as many as a hundred passengers. Pleasure steamers are a great feature of summer life on the Thames for there are beautiful and exciting places to see.

The first place the steamers reach is Henley.

This is a world-famous town, for it is here the international regattas are held. Here the best oarsmen from all over the world compete.

At the beginning of this century it was thought fashionable to own a boat. The most talked about town in that day was Maidenhead, near which was a lock called Boulter's. At the beginning of this century, Boulter's Lock was a place visited by crowds on Sundays. This was because actresses, especially those acting in musicals, lovely chorus girls and famous beauties used to have Sunday lunch at Maidenhead with their boyfriends. Afterwards they went on the river in motor launches, rowing boats and punts. The boats usually headed for Boulter's Lock.

Imagine the scene. Men in tight white flannels and striped blazers sported boaters. Ladies with huge hats, dresses of chiffon and lace were sheltered under frilly sunshades. People crowded

around the lock peering into it, trying to spot a favorite. Then suddenly a cry "Oh, look who's there!" "How you doing, Lily?" "'avin' a nice time, Gertie?"

After Maidenhead comes one of the great treats the river has to offer. Standing on a hill is Windsor Castle. To see the castle at its best is to see it rising from the mist in the morning or in the pink light of sunset. Then it looks as magical as Sleeping Beauty's palace looked to the Prince.

Another royal building on the Thames is Hampton Court Palace. This is where the pleasure steamers which start from London finish their trip upriver. In the summer, thousands of people visit Hampton Court for its historical interest. But children do not take the trip to Hampton Court Palace only because of its history. They visit it because of its maze, and because there is a haunted gallery where the ghost of Queen Catherine Howard, one of the wives of Henry VIII, is said to walk.

20

*A pleasure steamer passes Windsor Castle.*

The British Travel Association

*The maze at Hampton Court attracts many visitors.*

The maze is a sort of puzzle inside high hedges. There are many winding paths, and the game is to try to take the right ones to reach the center and then to get out again. Few people manage this without help. Usually they get hopelessly lost and are rescued by gardeners standing on ladders shouting directions.

Below Hampton Court the Thames comes to Teddington Lock. After this the river becomes tidal. It has the same tides as the North Sea, into which it later flows. Twice daily the tide sweeps up the Thames, and out again. It is because of these tides that the Thames has become rich and important.

Now that the river is tidal there are great changes to be seen. The City of London sprawls out to turn the river's banks from pleasure to business. There are shipyards, neon signs, new houses and bungalows and clusters of house trailers.

The traffic on the river changes too. Tugs towing laden barges and lighters (large open boats used for loading or unloading ships) chug their

*When the Thames reaches London, it becomes a busy river.*
British Official Photograph

way past rowing teams practicing for regattas.
Trainers of the teams rush up and down the
towpaths shouting directions through megaphones.
Large boathouses with names painted over them
show that big businesses have sporting clubs for
their employees. This means there are fleets of
rowing and sailing boats, for the various clubs
constantly compete against each other.

Here there are almost no wild birds on the
Thames and far fewer flowers on the banks. The
swans are still there, as regal as ever. Still, there
is a lot that is worth looking at, especially Syon
House. This is one of the great houses that
was built in the eighteenth century and is still
privately owned. It belongs to the Duke of
Northumberland. Birds who now find the Thames
and its banks too crowded to be comfortable
live on the splendid grounds of Syon House.

Facing Syon House are the Royal Botanical
Gardens, more often called Kew Gardens. About
25,000 different types of plants are grown here,
plus three million kinds of herbs. Kew Gardens

are beautiful all the year round, but particularly
so in the spring. For then the wild bluebells and
the flowering trees are in bloom, and no garden
has more perfect lilacs.

To many Londoners, especially the children, the
Thames means the Boat Race. This is an immensely popular free entertainment. Teams from
Oxford and Cambridge universities row in compe-
tition. The race starts at a town called Putney
and finishes at another called Mortlake, which is
downriver from Syon House. It is a hard race,
for the course is four and a quarter miles long.

*The Oxford-Cambridge Boat Race is one of London's favorites.*
The British Travel Association

Because it takes place in the early spring, it is often rowed in bad weather.

Following the crews in launches are the Old Blues, as they are called, for Oxford wears dark blue blazers and caps and Cambridge pale blue. Old Blues are the men who once rowed in the Boat Race. To be an Old Blue is to be among the elite of the rowing world. On the banks thousands congregate to cheer their favorites.

Probably not one in a hundred of those watching the Boat Race has ever visited either university, even for a day. But that does not prevent them from being strong supporters of one or the other team. They show their support by wearing enormous rosettes of either pale or dark blue. All free entertainments are popular with Londoners, but none is more popular than the Boat Race.

The river is now quite grown up. It is wide, strong and deep, well able to force its way to the sea. But it is still gentle enough for ships to anchor on it in safety. So now in quiet dignity the Thames comes to London.

*A quiet street in Chelsea.*

# 3. The Thames Comes to London

If the Thames traveled as straight as the crow is supposed to fly, it would journey only 40 miles through London to reach the North Sea. But becoming a Londoner has not changed its twisting, turning habit. As a result it travels 60 miles instead of 40 before it reaches the sea.

Another habit the Thames does not lose is collecting tributaries. London has many rivers, some now little more than underground streams. These join the Thames as it passes through

*Tugs, barges and pleasure boats move on "London's River."*

London and its suburbs. So when the river
reaches a sandbank called The Nore, which is
near the end of its journey, the Thames is ten
miles wide. Imagine that for a river which, not
so long ago, was called "The Brook."

Even in its early London life, the Thames is a
busy river. Barges towing fleets of lighters chug
up and down. Busy police boats dart by. But
alongside the working craft, pleasure boats still
have their place. In the summer, especially on

weekends, there is a constant flow of passenger steamers. There are private launches, rowing boats, even occasionally a sailing dinghy. And among the boats, there are the swans still serene and regal.

On its north bank one of the first places in London which the Thames passes is Chelsea. London is divided into boroughs, of which Chelsea is one. Each borough, though a part of London, is domestically self-governing. Also each borough has its own members of Parliament.

Chelsea has had a long history and is famous for many things. Among them are Chelsea buns, which are spiced strips of dough wound into a coil with frosting on top. At one time these were made in what was called a bun house, which was patronized by royalty. Nowadays all pastry cooks make them. Another thing Chelsea was famous for in the eighteenth century was its china. The Chelsea factory became world-renowned for its porcelain vases, candlesticks and other objects, which have since become valuable antiques.

At one time Chelsea was just a small village on the riverbank. King Charles II used to come there from his palace to bathe. He liked bathing in the Thames at Chelsea village so much that he ordered a private road to be made for him. To this day there is a King's Road in Chelsea, but everyone uses it now.

It is lovely to walk beside the Thames on its north bank along Chelsea Embankment. There it is possible to feel you are back in the eighteenth century. The houses look as they looked then, only now they are mellowed by age. Each has a beautiful front door with an ornate sky-light over it. Each house, as was possible in those more spacious days, is set in a garden among trees.

Also on the north bank of the river are the lovely grounds of Chelsea Hospital, a home for old soldiers. The hospital was built by Sir Christopher Wren, the great architect who rebuilt much of London after the fire in 1666.

On the south bank there is a gigantic fun fair, or amusement park, and a public park. In 1951 the English held the Festival of Britain to show the world the things Great Britain could make and do. But people who come to festivals also want to be amused, so a fun fair was erected. This was gay and pretty to look at. It was built on the riverbank so that it could be reached from the Festival proper, which was downriver. The fun fair was such a success that it has been open every summer since then, and it adds a gay if noisy touch to life on the riverbank.

In the nineteenth century Chelsea became the home of artists of all descriptions. Some of the painters who lived there were Rossetti, Turner and Whistler. The writers Carlyle, Henry James and Mrs. Gaskell also made Chelsea their home.

The Thames leaves Chelsea to enter the City of Westminster. Westminster is another borough and a royal one. Westminster was royal even in the fourteenth century when it was a village. It has remained royal because the reigning monarch has always had a home in the borough of Westminster. There have been various palaces, two of them on the riverbank. Buckingham Palace is in Westminster but not near the river.

On its north bank the river comes into the borough of Westminster by passing a wide road called Millbank. Here is the Tate Gallery, which houses one of the nation's finest collections of pictures.

The House of Commons, on the riverbank, has a beautiful terrace beside the water where members of Parliament and their guests can sit. In the tower above is a clock with a world-famous bell to sound the hours. It is called Big Ben.

Across the river is the borough of Lambeth. Here is Lambeth Palace. This is the London home of the Archbishop of Canterbury. It belongs to the days when there was room to house the great in style and dignity.

Beyond Lambeth Palace grounds is one of London's great hospitals. It is called St. Thomas's and is on the Thames bank. It was built in seven pavilions from a plan of Florence Nightingale's. The hospital was severely damaged by enemy

*Big Ben is the great bell in the clock tower.*

action during World War II and is to be rebuilt. But Florence Nightingale's original design is considered so good that its plan is being followed in the rebuilding.

Now the Thames flows past the County Hall. This is a building which was new at the beginning of this century. It has a splendid terrace frontage giving an unrivaled view of the river. Those who govern all the boroughs that make up London work inside County Hall.

Back across the river is Westminster Pier. It is from here that most of the pleasure steamers start their journeys up and down the river. All

*Pleasure boats load passengers for a river cruise.*

summer long lines of pleasure-seekers wait to go aboard. The children going upriver chatter expectantly about the maze and the haunted gallery at Hampton Court Palace.

A wide thoroughfare called the Victoria Embankment now runs along the riverbank. The first building of importance on the embankment is New Scotland Yard. This is the headquarters of London's police force. It is called Scotland Yard because once there was a palace where the Yard now stands. This was the London home of Scottish kings before England and Scotland were made into one kingdom.

Against the wall, which is on the river side of the Victoria Embankment, is a strange sight. It is an Egyptian obelisk, a tall, slender pillar. It is called Cleopatra's Needle, though it had nothing to do with Cleopatra. It is one of two obelisks that were built about 1,450 years before Christ was born. The obelisks had a varied history. One was finally brought to London in the nineteenth century to be erected where it now

*Cleopatra's Needle, in the foreground, faces the Royal Festival Hall across the river in London.*

stands. A year later the other obelisk was sent to New York. Cleopatra's Needle, which is of pink granite, looks especially odd in London, where the over-all coloring is silver-gray.

Facing the Needle across the river is the Royal Festival Hall. This was the main building of the 1951 Festival when the fun fair was first erected. It is very modern and looks magical at night when it is a blaze of light. It is a concert hall and the home of a ballet company. It also has lecture rooms and a huge restaurant overlooking the river. In summer after dark the Royal Festival Hall is linked on both the south and north banks by chains of lights. These, reflected in the Thames, look like jeweled necklaces. In front of the hall is the pier from which steamers carry passengers upriver to the fun fair.

Across the Thames against the Victoria Embankment is a floating police station. Most of London's police stations have flower-growing competitions each summer. The floating police station is as gay as a land police station, for it has window boxes and tubs of flowers on its floating dock.

The river police boats are always busy on the London Thames, for as well as seeing to law and order they have another job. This is to keep the river clear of flotsam. An enormous amount of flotsam, which is mostly floating wood, washes upriver on each tide. Riverside dwellers also gather flotsam to sell.

Now the Thames is leaving Westminster to enter "The City." It is about to start the busiest part of its life.

*River police are now equipped with fiberglass launches.*

*Sculptured lions are to be seen everywhere in London.*

# 4. The Thames Goes to Work

In the heart of London is one square mile called The City. The City is ruled by the Lord Mayor of London. It has its own police force. It is today, and was from London's beginnings, the commercial center of the country. It is said to be the most important square mile in the world.

Inside The City are many world-famous buildings. Here is the Bank of England. The bank is known as "The Old Lady of Threadneedle Street." This is because there is the figure of a woman on the front of the building, and because the bank faces Threadneedle Street. The City also houses

St. Paul's Cathedral, the Stock Exchange and the Tower of London.

The Lord Mayor of London lives in the Mansion House. Each year there is a big parade when the newly elected Lord Mayor rides through The City in a gold coach. There are also floats representing some subject in which the Lord Mayor is interested. In the past the Lord Mayor's procession was on the water. This Thames event was most splendid in the seventeenth century. The Lord Mayor's gorgeous, ornate barge was followed by decorated boats belonging to the City Fathers. The Lord Mayor's Show is another of those free entertainments beloved by the Londoners.

The Lord Mayor the children know best is Dick Whittington. According to the legend, Dick ran away from London, where he had been cruelly treated. As he was resting on the road outside the city, he heard the chiming church bells. They seemed to say, "Turn again, Whittington, thrice Lord Mayor of London." So he turned back and was three times Lord Mayor, in 1397, 1406 and

*Dick Whittington is the Lord Mayor best known to children.*

1419. What the history books do not say, but what every child knows, is that Dick Whittington had a cat.

One of the first buildings the Thames flows by as it reaches The City is new to London. It is a theater called the Mermaid. The theater restaurant is built right on the river. Diners can watch ships passing up and down, tugs towing rows of lighters, barges, police boats and, in the summer, pleasure steamers. And again, there are the swans, cruising as majestically as they did when they lorded it among the water birds.

Different areas of The City are famous for particular things. The Thames reaches the furriers' quarter, one of the many foreign areas. The names over the warehouses are hard for the British to pronounce.

Now the Thames comes to Billingsgate where London's great fish market is located. Up to a century ago the Thames was full of fish. At one time even salmon could be caught there. Now pollution has put an end to the fish, but the market remains. Today fish are sent to the market largely by land from all around the coast, and from the rivers.

Billingsgate porters, who carry the fish, wear special hats. These are called "billycocks." They are supposed to be modeled after the helmets of the archers who fought at the Battle of Agincourt. The market is believed to date back to the days when the Romans occupied Britain.

Today there are wharves and warehouses facing

*The Billingsgate porter's flat-topped hat helps to support his load of fish.*

Billingsgate across the river. But it was not always so. In the sixteenth century it was a great place for amusements. Here was the Globe Theatre, in which Shakespeare's plays were first acted. Here too were buildings used for what was then called sport—bull- and bear-baiting, and cockfighting.

Among today's wharves is one called Clink which is built where once stood a notorious prison called by that name. It was closed in the seventeenth century, but to this day the British slang for being sent to prison is "sent to clink."

Now on the other bank the Thames has reached the Tower of London. This building is well known to the river which has carried so many through the Traitors' Gate. Although the water gate is no longer used, to see it still sends shivers down one's spine. It is terrible to remember how many who were rowed through the gate lost their heads on the block.

Today, except in time of war, the Tower is not used as a prison. It is an armory and the crown jewels are kept there. The Tower has a governor called the Constable of the Tower. He has a small garrison under his command, as well as yeomen warders. The warders are more often called "beefeaters" for there was a time when a part of their pay was beef. The beefeaters look most picturesque for they are dressed exactly as they were in the reign of Henry VII.

At the Tower live some old acquaintances of the Thames—the ravens. There is a legend that

44

when there are no ravens at the Tower the British Commonwealth will come to an end. These evil-looking birds are suitable residents for that blood-soaked place. But in spite of its grisly past, the floodlit Tower on a summer's night looks magical beyond belief.

Past the Tower, the Thames becomes a seaman's river. From there on, it carries deep-sea ships. It has now left The City and is entering London's east end.

The Thames is now in dockland—miles of piers on both banks to serve the multitudes of ships which dock there. The stores for these docks hold goods from every corner of the world. Anything and everything that ships can carry and merchants can sell can be found on the Thames' docks.

In dockland every inch of river frontage is so valuable that there are no houses or footpaths. So it is only when they travel by water that the public can see the river. There are exceptions. One is the old smuggling inn, "The Prospect of

*"The Prospect of Whitby," built in 1520, still stands on the banks of the Thames.*

Whitby." Nowadays this is a popular "pub," or tavern. But the Thames can remember the days when boats drew in under its balcony to pass smuggled goods up through a trapdoor.

When it is possible to get a view of the Thames, one can see cargo boats and tramp steamers from all over the world. At the borough of Deptford there are great timber yards where wood is stored, brought from the forests of Scandinavia and Canada. It was in the borough of Deptford that Sir Walter Raleigh is said to have laid down his cloak for Queen Elizabeth I.

*The* CUTTY SARK, *a nineteenth century tea clipper, is now in dry dock at Greenwich.*

Now the Thames reaches the borough of Greenwich. This is the downriver end of the trip by pleasure steamer. Here, resting after an arduous sea life, is the *Cutty Sark*. She was a famous sailing ship. One of her cargoes was tea from Australia. At the end of the last century there used to be great races by the tea clippers to be up the Thames first, and so get the top price for tea. The *Cutty Sark* was a great racer in her day; now thousands go to visit her.

As the river passes the eastern boroughs of London, the scene along the Thames changes. The built-up areas became fewer as the marshes begin. Barking Creek, where London's refuse is brought to be turned into sludge, is in this area. The sludge is either scattered on fields or taken by sludge boat to be dumped into the open sea.

The desolate marshlands stretch for miles, broken only occasionally by industrial plants. Finally the river reaches Tilbury, the port from which passenger liners sail for Australia, New Zealand and the Far East.

Now there is a smell of the sea in the air. But though the river is crowded, the banks grow ever more lonely. For there are nothing but mud flats split up by creeks. But if the flats are lonely for human beings they are not lonely for birds. There are herring gulls, ducks, oyster catchers, bar-tailed godwits, ringed plovers, dunlins, redshanks and knots. Here too are the sea flowers—horn poppies, sea campions, thrift, sea cabbage, sea lavender and sea purslane. Although nowadays these mud flats belong only to wildlife, there was a time, and not so long ago, when the flats were the haunt of smugglers.

The flats come to an end and the seaside towns begin. Canvey Island, a small holiday resort, is built on reclaimed land. Leigh-on-Sea, famous for its cockles, brings to mind the English song, "Cockles and mussels alive, alive oh!" Then comes Southend, an immensely popular, noisy seaside resort. Then Shoeburyness and Sheerness appear—both pleasant in the summer but bitterly cold and windswept in the winter.

The Thames is now ten miles wide—a tremendous river carrying on its broad reaches a huge volume of shipping. It has still a few miles to travel before it loses itself in the North Sea— a few miles during which sailors from all over the world call it affectionately, "London's river."

*A bittern hides itself among reeds along the riverbank.*

Annan Photo Features

*Roman soldiers in ancient England.*

# 5. Early History

Waterways are an important means of communication. But they also prevent communication unless there is some means of fording or crossing them. So on the Thames the places that have the most history are places where the river could be crossed.

The first place from the source where a crossing could easily be made is Wallingford in Berkshire. Today the Thames wanders through this village at the end of its period as a country river. But here once was a thriving garrison town on which many roads converged. What armies have waded

*Wallingford was once a thriving garrison town.*

across the Thames at Wallingford—Britons, Romans, Saxons, Danes and Normans.

There were other places where it was believed the river could be forded on occasion. One was at the village of Westminster.

It was the Romans who turned a little settlement called Lyn Din into a flourishing city. They called it Londinium. They were smart people and saw at once the value of the tidal Thames. But to be of value it must be crossed. So they built a wooden bridge, which was a great feat. This was on the best site they could find. It was

53

roughly where a bridge called London Bridge stands today.

Watling Street, one of the earliest of the great Roman roads, passes through London. The Romans had a genius for road building; many of their roads are in use today. Sometimes the British wish they could come back and show us how they built them.

It is clear, too, the Romans made a fine job of popularizing the Thames. They must have regulated the shipping, probably charging dues and customs for their trouble. They certainly must have dredged the river and built quays. For a famous Roman historian called Tacitus reported that the pool of Londinium was thronged with merchant and trading vessels.

The final Roman invasion was in A.D. 43. At this time the dockland part of the Thames was something like it is today. That is to say, boats were coming in carrying everything the merchants could sell. Outward they took everything Britain had to market. One cargo would certainly have been slaves. Another is believed to have been oysters, as oysters from Britain had become a delicacy in Rome.

Then in A.D. 61 Londinium suffered a setback. No matter how much prosperity the invaders brought, some of the British hated them. One of these was a British queen called Boadicea. She, fighting to free Britain from the occupying Roman legions, attacked Londinium and burned it.

The Romans took back what was left of the city. They rebuilt it and Londinium settled down to a period of peace and prosperity. It lasted 400 years. And the Thames grew more important and carried more shipping.

Around the year A.D. 433, the power of Rome began to fade. This information would have reached Londinium by rumors brought there by seamen. Up and down the banks of the Thames the gossip would be whispered. Could it be true? Was mighty Rome falling apart? But soon the truth became visible. For from all over the country the legions were on the march. Many crossed the Thames to reach the coast to embark for home. Others sailed from the Thames.

Life was hard after the Romans left. This was because of the Saxons. These rough invaders had long been making raids on Britain. Now that the Roman legions had gone, the Saxons increased their raids. They trebled their efforts. In the end they conquered the Britons. The Saxon period in Britain was a dark one. But light was coming.

In 597, the monk Augustine was sent by Rome as a Christian missionary to the Britons. He landed on the Isle of Thanet. This is south of the Thames mouth. He preached Christianity. The result was that in less than 100 years Britain became a Christian country. Monasteries were built. Three were on the Thames banks. Up and down the country churches were erected. Some of these Saxon churches can still be seen from the Thames. Britain, or England as she was now called, became civilized, for under the monks many people were educated. The monks also taught better farming methods.

*The village of Abingdon grew up around a Benedictine abbey built in the seventh century.*

But prosperity was dangerous, and the monasteries were very prosperous indeed. They possessed great riches, including rich vestments and gold ornaments. Then from the north the Vikings, a warlike people who still worshipped their own gods, swept down in terrible raids, destroying the monasteries—burning, murdering, pillaging. Many a dead body must have been thrown into the Thames in those ghastly years. The English fought back. Led by King Alfred, who was supposed to have burned the cakes, and other kings, the English waged constant war on the Danish raiders. But the Danes were a savage people, and it was a period of fear and uneasiness.

Yet a little more than a hundred years later a fine Danish king called Canute was ruling England. Canute was a great administrator and brought peace to the land. But it is not because he ruled well that he is remembered by English children. They know him as the king who was told he could rule the waves of the sea. It is said that he decided the only way to teach his courtiers not to talk stupidly was to show them how wrong they were. He had a stool carried to the water's edge. On this he sat, his crown on his head, his sceptre in his hand. Then, in his most royal voice, he ordered the waves to go back. Of course the waves did nothing of the sort. But it was not until he was very wet that his courtiers accepted that the waves had won.

With the dawning of better times the monasteries that had been destroyed were rebuilt. Once more there was education and a better way of life. A king called Edward the Confessor rebuilt the Abbey of Westminster, which had been burned. He also built himself a wooden palace at Windsor.

Now the people began to unite. Romans, Saxons and Vikings all called themselves English. It was during this period of peace that settlements were formed up the Thames. Many of these were the beginnings of the towns and villages the river passes through today.

London became prosperous once more. Trade became brisk. Loaded ships sailed in on each tide, and others equally loaded sailed out. From across the Channel, England appeared to William of Normandy to be a ripe fruit ready to be eaten.

In 1066, William of Normandy invaded England. There, after a bloody battle near Hastings, he beat the English, killing their king, who was called Harold. After he had won the battle of Hastings, William led his troops to conquer London. As it turned out, London did not fight,

but surrendered to William. In exchange London accepted a charter guaranteeing her freedom.

William of Normandy, now called William the Conqueror, built himself a castle just outside the old Roman city wall. This he called La Blaunche Tour (The White Tower). This tower is now the center of the Tower of London. He also replaced the wooden castle at Windsor with a stone one.

Among the many changes that came about under William the Conqueror was the use of stone for buildings. Along the banks of the Thames, stone churches and mansions began to rise.

London Bridge, which had been built and re-built since the Roman original, was reconstructed of stone. It had to be very strong to withstand the volumes of water shooting under it with the ebb and flow of each tide. This stone bridge was to stand for 700 years.

The new bridge was a very popular place on which to live. Shops with living quarters above them were packed on both sides of the bridge.

*Aerial view of the Tower of London. In the center is the White Tower. Tower Bridge is in the foreground.*

The British Travel Association

This resulted in a lot of traffic on London's only bridge. It must also have been extremely noisy for the householders. Imagine the shouts of drivers trying to pass each other, the clip-clop of the horses' feet and the roar of the river below.

Those lucky enough to get a house on the bridge would not have worried about noise for they had comforts denied other Londoners. They had no need for a horrible main drain running down the middle of their street into which all waste was thrown. These street drains resulted in terrible smells and often plague. Bridge dwellers got rid of their rubbish by tipping it into the Thames. Besides, they were spared fetching and paying for water, as did other Londoners. They had only to lower buckets for what they needed. The bridge houses were healthy, for good clean air blew in at the windows. And, of course, the inhabitants had an unrivaled view of the river and the shipping.

The stone London Bridge had twenty pointed

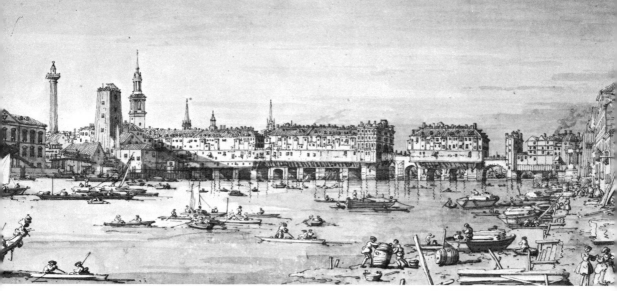

*Drawing of the old London Bridge by Canaletto.*

arches. One of these had a wooden drawbridge which could be raised when an exceptionally tall ship needed to sail up the river. The bridge was so constructed that it greatly reduced the force of the river above the bridge. This gave a wide calm reach which stretched as far as the village of Westminster. This meant that in cold years the river here froze so hard that an ox could be roasted whole on the ice. Frost Fairs were held at which there were booths and tents selling food and souvenirs. And there were sports: bull-baiting, horse racing, coach racing and the other amusements of the period, such as puppet shows.

One of England's major historical events did not occur in London but at Runnymede, which is upriver between Staines and Windsor. This was the acceptance of Magna Carta by King John in 1215. Magna Carta was a charter giving remarkable rights to free Englishmen. King John would not have signed such a charter of his free will. He was forced to sign by a group of barons who, when the king proved stubborn, chose a leader and marched on London.

During the Middle Ages the river was to a large extent the center of London life. The monarch would travel from the Tower to Westminster in a grand barge, as did the Lord Mayor when he was newly appointed. Since there was only one bridge, it was usual to travel by water. The well-to-do had their own barges and boats, the less well-off hired theirs. To be a Thames boatman plying for hire was quite a prosperous job in those days.

On the riverbanks poverty and riches rubbed shoulders, for the rich were very rich and the poor were desperately poor. The health conditions were deplorable. The Thames was filthy and there were frequent attacks of plague and other dreadful diseases. Too often Londoners saw the carts going round The City collecting the dead to be tossed into plague pits. At that time deaths exceeded births. Country people moving into town, and immigrants arriving from abroad kept the population about even.

But upriver the population was growing. This was because rich wool and cloth merchants built houses there. They probably moved partly to get out of unhealthy London. But in the Cotswold Hills they moved to be near the sheep farmers. For the source of their wealth was sheep. Many of these merchants were fabulously wealthy. They were lavish spenders and left their mark wherever they settled. They built beautiful churches and laid out exquisite towns. Towns such as Lechlade are now of small importance. But they still stand, monuments to an age that spent unsparingly on beauty.

The British Travel Association

*Lechlade is now a sleepy little town. Beyond this point the Thames is no longer navigable.*

When London was given its freedom by William the Conqueror, The City became very independent. London's power was also increased because The City owned the London Militia.

In the Middle Ages every town had militia. These were men who guarded towns from enemies. It was accepted by all that life was dangerous. As a result each man was glad to help defend his liberties. Naturally, since it was The City square mile in which most people lived, it was from there London's militia was conscripted. So it came under the control of the Lord Mayor and the rich citizens. This gave the Lord Mayor powers denied even to the King.

Kings had no place in London. This meant that when the reigning monarch wanted to come near The City he skirted it. He stayed either in his White Tower below The City, or his palace at Westminster above it.

To this day the ancient rights of The City are preserved. No reigning monarch may enter it without the permission of the Lord Mayor. When the Queen goes into The City, her car stops at a spot still called Temple Bar, though now there is no bar there but only a statue of a griffin to mark the entrance to The City. There the Lord Mayor meets her and gives her permission to drive on.

It must not be thought that in the Middle Ages peace and prosperity were all that the Thames knew. There was intermittent war with France for a hundred years. Then in the fifteenth century there was a civil war called the Wars of the Roses. This was to decide which great royal family should inherit the throne. As their emblem one side wore the white rose and the other the red. The war began on the Thames embankment between Westminster and The City. There, the two royal dukes met in a garden and quarrelled. In the garden there were roses. One snatched a white rose and the other a red. Both declared war.

But in spite of wars England prospered. This was especially due to her wool trade and to the Thames which carried both wool to London and finished material to the world. Because England prospered, the Thames saw great refinements in the way the people lived. And it was to see still greater changes.

*An old sailing vessel anchored in the Thames.*
The British Travel Association

# 6. Tudor England

Kings and queens have surnames. Tudor was the surname of Henry VII, Henry VIII, Edward VI, Queen Mary and Queen Elizabeth I. While the Tudors were on the throne there was great expansion in all things artistic. So Tudor England made a great difference to the life of those who lived on the banks of the Thames. But the Tudors brought bad things, too.

The Tower of London played a big part in Tudor history. The White Tower, built by William the Conqueror, was in Tudor times the center of a vast state prison. This was surrounded by a

69

*The Tower of London and, in the foreground, Traitors' Gate.*

moat. A watergate, called the Traitors' Gate, gave access to the Thames. Inside was a network of prison cells and dungeons. The whole fortress was surrounded by a high wall.

The Tower has a bloody history, for many heads were chopped off there. But other crimes were committed. Two little princes, Edward V and his brother, were murdered there in 1483, and many people suffered long imprisonments, including two kings of Scotland and one of France.

70

When Henry VIII came to the throne, the Thames carried many people through the Traitors' Gate. It must have been a gloomy journey by water, knowing how it might well end. Imagine being rowed to your probable death down a river on which luckier people were skimming to and fro on business and pleasure.

One of the many passengers to be carried through the Traitors' Gate was Anne Boleyn. She was the second wife of Henry VIII. Her journey to the Tower must have been particularly sad, for she had been married there. She was beheaded in 1536. Six years later Henry's fifth wife, Catherine Howard, met the same fate. She is the Queen who is supposed to haunt Hampton Court.

During Henry VIII's reign, the wealthy monasteries vanished from England. There were many reasons why Henry expelled the monks. One was greed. The monasteries and convents were immensely rich and Henry wanted money. Another reason was that Henry quarrelled with the Pope. He severed the country's connection with Rome and established Protestantism in England. Those Catholics who disapproved—and there were many —were too often rowed to their death through the Traitors' Gate.

It was during Henry VIII's reign that Hampton Court Palace was built. Before the monasteries were closed, Henry had a powerful counselor called Cardinal Wolsey. Cardinal Wolsey had so many positions that he became enormously rich, and so grand he seemed almost as powerful as the King. His personal household was made up of

*Hampton Court Palace was originally built for Cardinal Wolsey.*

over 500 people. No wonder he needed a palace to live in.

Hampton Court Palace is built in a beautiful garden divided into courts. Inside the palace are magnificent State apartments. Today there are 500 pictures on exhibition. Long galleries lead to the suites of rooms. It is amazing to remember that this vast place was not built for a king.

Hampton Court must have been a sight to see when Wolsey was in residence. Imagine him arriving by road, magnificent in his crimson Cardinal's robe. Behind him followed his retinue of 500. All would be richly dressed—a riot of color. In Henry's reign men as well as women wore colorful, elegant clothing. Wolsey's arrival was a pageant for the curtseying, hat-doffing villagers.

But Wolsey, like many an ambitious man, had a sad end. He was supposed to go to the Tower to be beheaded. He never reached there. He died of disease and, some say, a broken heart on the way. Before he died he said to the Lieutenant of the

73

Tower of London who had taken him into custody, "Had I but served my God as diligently as I have served the King, He would not have given me over in my gray hairs."

Wolsey's power grew less, so before the great palace was even finished, he gave it as a gift to the King. For the next two centuries it was a royal residence. Today, though it is still a royal palace, commoners live there. Apartments are loaned by the monarch to distinguished people as a reward for service to the State. They are known as Grace and Favour apartments.

When Henry VIII died, he was followed on the throne by his daughter Mary. She was called "Bloody Mary," for during her reign many heads rolled off the Tower block. One of the most pathetic deaths was Lady Jane Grey's. She was seventeen, of royal blood, and her father tried to claim the throne for her. Instead, Mary ordered her death.

Mary, a devout Roman Catholic, attempted during her reign to restore Catholicism to England.

But the Protestants, under a leader called Sir Thomas Wyatt, stormed London and very nearly won The City. Then Mary rode into The City and appealed to the citizens to stand by their Queen. That must have been quite an occasion. And she did win The City back.

After Wyatt's uprising the executioner worked overtime. One head was no sooner off than another was lying on the block ready for the ax. The Thames saw some horrid sights. Unimportant people who had followed Wyatt were not considered worthy of the block. Instead, they were hung. Many a body must have swung in the wind on the Thames' banks.

One fine day a sumptuous barge came upriver to London. At the prow gleamed a great cross. In the boat sat the Pope's representative. He was met by members of Parliament, looking respectful and probably humble. It must have seemed that day as if Mary and Catholicism had won.

But as usual The City could not be forced. The citizens might have been temporarily carried away by a speech from a brave Queen, but in the end they made their own decisions. They proved so stubborn that many laws Mary would like to have made had to be abandoned. Moreover, there were strong characters among the Protestants who were not afraid of death. Two of the most famous met their end upriver at Oxford.

A Protestant reformer called Latimer and a Bishop Ridley were ordered to be burned at the stake. Latimer, as the flames billowed up around him, called out, "Play the man, Master Ridley. We shall this day light such a flame in England as I trust shall never be put out." And he was quite right. He and men like him lived on in people's hearts. And in any case, even the most devout Catholics were sick of bloodshed.

Elizabeth I, a Protestant, was 25 when she became Queen. She was beautiful, intelligent and well educated. Above all, she was every inch a Queen. Like her father she loved splendor and amusement. It was her pleasure to move with her court from stately home to stately home. For

*No one today is sure of exactly how the Globe Theater was built. It is thought to have been similar to the drawing above.*

this reason there are many homes today which have a bed with a notice that says "Queen Elizabeth slept here." She also loved music and poetry. In her reign the arts flourished as never before.

It was during the reign of Elizabeth that Shakespeare wrote his plays. They were acted in London at the Globe and other theaters. Theater companies, highly trained and respected, also visited the great houses. The Thames must have seen many a procession of actors going across

London's bridge on their way to visit a rich patron. And innumerable citizens crossed the Thames by the bridge or by boat to visit the theaters. What roars of laughter rang across the water at the antics of the clowns! How silent was the audience as the glorious poetry swelled over them! For poetry at that date was every man's language.

Now to Westminster. By Tudor times there were two Houses of Parliament—the Lords and the Commons. The royal palace was away from the river in a part of Westminster called Whitehall. So the House of Lords in Elizabeth's reign met in part of that palace built by Edward the Confessor. The Commons met in a place called St. Stephen's Chapel. So, though the royal home had moved, it was still in Westminster, and Westminster was still the center of government. The buildings where the members sat were placed side by side with the Abbey, as they are today.

The Thames had watched great changes in the governing of the country. It was Elizabeth's idea, and that of her father and sister, that she, rather than Parliament, should rule. She called the members together very seldom and then only when she wanted something. But the members had different views. They pressed firmly on towards governing the country themselves. Especially was this true of the lower house called the Commons.

It was during the reign of Elizabeth that the eyes of Englishmen were turned to the New World. Many ships sailed from the west country to America carrying settlers, goods and men in search of gold. But what the Thames saw of America was in new cargoes—the tobacco and potatoes. These would have been brought from the west country by coastal boats up Channel, and so up the Thames.

But one party of merchant adventurers sailed from the Thames to America. This was in 1606. There, at Jamestown, Virginia, they founded the first permanent British colony. It was at Jamestown that John Rolfe married Pocahontas.

There is a memorial to these settlers at the entrance to the East India Dock.

After Elizabeth died a king called James came to the throne. During his reign something happened in Westminster village, which English children remember and celebrate each year. The old quarrel between Protestants and Roman Catholics had never died. Desperate for their cause, some Roman Catholics made a plot. They put barrels of gunpowder under the House of Commons.

The idea was that when the King next summoned Parliament, which would be on November 5, he and his Parliament would be blown sky-high together. A soldier of fortune named Guido Fawkes was hired to set off the gunpowder.

The plot was discovered and the planners hanged, drawn and quartered. But to this day every November 5 is remembered as Guy Fawkes Day. For weeks beforehand bonfires are built. Images of Guy Fawkes are made. These are exhibited for money, which is spent on fireworks. Then, on the night of November 5, fireworks blaze

*Above, children gather with their Guy Fawkeses on November 5.*
*Below, burning an old ship on Guy Fawkes Day is traditional in Rye, Sussex.*

from one end of the country to the other. The Guys are burned on the bonfires. It is a great children's night.

> *"Please to remember the fifth of November,*
> *The gunpowder treason and plot.*
> *I see no reason why gunpowder treason*
> *Should ever be forgot."*

After James, Charles I came to the throne. The Thames saw much sadness in that reign for there was a civil war. It was fought between the King's party, called the Cavaliers, and the Roundheads, who were commanded by Oliver Cromwell. After many bloody battles Charles I was captured. He was executed outside his palace in Whitehall.

What scenes the Thames witnessed during those sad years! Son fought against father, brother against brother. Old family friends were forced to betray each other. How many people hid among the reeds by the Thames? How many shared the shelter of the mudbanks with the sea birds? How many thousands hurried over London's bridge or by boat to see their King beheaded? How soon they were scurrying back, the men white-faced, the women in tears!

It was in the reign of Charles II that the face of London was changed by fire. The fire followed six months of dreadful plague. In those months a hundred thousand Londoners died. The court moved upriver to Oxford. Indeed, all who could got out of the city.

For those who stayed life was almost unbearable. If you had plague in the house a cross was chalked on your door. This meant no one was permitted to come near you. Carts were driven up and down the narrow cobbled streets. The drivers rang bells and shouted "Bring out your dead!" Coffins and shrouds soon gave out. There were few private graves. The dead were thrown into the carts to be tossed into plague pits.

The terrible fire which followed the plague destroyed the city. Thirteen thousand houses and ninety churches were burned to the ground. And what was lost in the docks is past computing. But a new seventeenth-century city rose from the ashes—a city which was to stand for 275 years until 1940 when it was again destroyed, this time by enemy action. During both fires the citizens saw the Thames as a river of gold in the light of the flames and saw a new city built on the ruins. But the seventeenth-century citizens were to see more than a new city rising from the smoke. They were to see a new people.

*Sailboats after a race in the Pool of London. In the background is Tower Bridge.*

*A London
lamplighter*

# 7.  From Then to Now

It was not only houses and churches that were built after the fire.  There were bridges.  One bridge and a ford or two were not enough for the new London.

The bridges did not come all at once.  But presently there were enough bridges to take care of all London's traffic.  There were also tunnels under the river.  This meant that the citizens no longer needed boats.  So gradually the barges were put away and the watermen who plied for hire disappeared.

Then the boats which sailed up the Thames

changed. The great sailing ships which had traveled the world vanished. In their place came what were then called iron ships. For now it was an age of steam.

There were vast changes too in land travel. The cavalcades of horses the Thames knew disappeared—as did almost all horse-drawn vehicles. Now it was the motor age. Motorcars, motor buses, motor bicycles scurried across the bridges and up the embankments. Now sometimes the shadow of an airplane was reflected in the water. Often the Thames saw a helicopter, for one used the grass near the Festival Theater on which to land.

The architecture has changed greatly. The great houses have become hotels, schools or other public buildings. The miles of slums below The City on the river's banks have disappeared. In their place apartment and office buildings have risen. Skyscrapers advertise to passing shipping the firm to which they belong.

One of the great changes seen by the Thames

is in the clothes worn by the male citizens. Back in the days of Charles II men wore gay, colorful clothes in velvets, satins and furs. But by the nineteenth century all that glory was gone. Men wore black clothes and, in The City, a top hat. Today dress is less formal than it was in the nineteenth century, but still there is a lot of black to be seen. Sometimes the Thames must sigh for the more colorful days it once knew.

Another change the Thames must notice is in the noise. It was always a noisy river, but the sounds have changed. Most of the cobblestones with which London's streets were paved have gone. These were terribly noisy as carts and carriages bounced over them, the horses' hooves clattering. Gone, too, are the street cries for which London was famous. But in their place there is the unending roar of London's traffic, the scream of jet planes overhead and the clatter of trains as they cross the Thames by railway bridge.

Another change is in health. In the past, few parents expected to raise all their children. In

London the chances of living to adulthood were poor. Now, with good sanitation and care of health, most people live to be adults.

But if great changes have been seen in the last hundred years, some things remain to remind the Thames of the past. Take, for example, the swans who have been on the Thames from its earliest days. You will remember how they looked down their beaks as if to say "We ought to wear crowns." Well, so they ought, for many of them are royal birds.

Every summer since the fourteenth century a ceremony called swan-upping takes place. Two of the old City Guilds, the Dyers and the Vintners, have the right to keep swans on the Thames.

Each Guild sends a boat up the Thames. In the boats, flying the Guild flags, are the Swan Wardens and men called Uppers. It is the business of the Uppers to make a nick on the beak of their cygnets (baby swans) born that spring. The Dyers make one nick, the Vintners two nicks.

But in charge of the swan-upping is the

*The Dyers and Vintners begin yearly marking of baby swans.*

Keeper of the Queen's Swans. He wears royal livery and he has with him a clipper. It is, of course, the Keeper of the Queen's Swans who decides which cygnet belongs to whom. The Queen's cygnets are not nicked, they merely have their wings clipped. It's no wonder swans look proud! No other water birds are looked after by a royal keeper, plus two City Guilds.

Back in the eighteenth century a regatta was held on the Thames. Among the races was one

*The boat of Her Majesty's Swankeeper carries a special flag.*

for watermen. A prize of ten guineas, a coat and a badge were presented by an actor called Doggett. Now, though watermen as such hardly exist, the race is still rowed. So each year somebody wins the money and an eighteenth century coat and badge as well. Though there are no watermen plying for hire today, the winner of Doggett's coat and badge is still greatly admired.

Another reminder of the days that are gone is the Royal Barge Master. He was actually used a few years ago. The Queen had been for a tour in the royal yacht. On her return the yacht was anchored in the Thames. So, to the joy of the citizens, the river was used as it used to be. Ships, bridges and landing stages were decorated, and the Queen came ashore in the royal barge. This was, of course, under the charge of the Royal Barge Master and his staff. The Londoners cheered themselves hoarse, because it was so splendid to see once more pageantry on the Thames.

But if there is little pageantry nowadays on the water there is plenty on the banks of the Thames. Most of this is at Westminster, but some takes us to that fairy tale palace the Thames passed when it was a pleasure river—Windsor Castle. Though the building was begun by William the Conqueror and looks like an early fortress, the private apartments inside are quite modern. For it is here that the Queen and her household spend their weekends much of the year. But the great pageantry of Windsor is now largely confined to funerals.

When Queen Victoria's husband Prince Albert died, a chapel was erected in his memory. For the last 150 years monarchs have been buried under this chapel. Queen Victoria and her husband were not buried there but in the grounds. Yet it was Queen Victoria's funeral which forever has added a touch of color to royal funerals. She was buried on a bitter winter's day. When the coffin was placed on the gun carriage to be pulled up to the castle the horses slipped. They could not get a grip on the icy road. So a party of sailors were ordered to cut the horses' traces and pull the gun carriage. Ever since then, sailors have drawn their monarch's body to its last resting place.

Does the Thames remember? Those early settlers whose primitive arrows are found in the river gravel. The Romans who built London and its first bridge. The monks who lived on its banks, after Augustine brought Christianity to England.

The Vikings who stained the Thames' water with blood. Edward the Confessor rebuilding Westminster Abbey. The coming of William the

*Sailors pull the gun carriage carrying the coffin of George VI.*

Conqueror. The people who lived on the first stone London Bridge. King John being forced to accept Magna Carta at Runnymede. The great river processions, especially the Lord Mayor's. The sad people who were rowed through the Traitors' Gate. William Shakespeare hurrying to a rehearsal. The poetry that was spoken and the songs which were sung.

The black day when a King lost his head. The golden day when the exiled Charles II returned in triumph to London. The cry of the men in charge of the plague carts. The flickering flames

93

when London burned. The rustling silks. The sedan chairs. The first motorcar.

Does it remember the children? Children of all dates who knew there was nothing so much fun as messing about in boats. The river birds who lived, and live, on and by the water. The flowers that have covered its banks.

Does it cling to its last moment as the Thames? Is it glad as it merges into the North Sea to hear sailors say, "There is London's river"?

British Information Services

# Index

# Meet the Author

NOEL STREATFEILD writes: "Believe it or not, I took to writing books because I thought it was a safe career. I was an actress . . . touring Australia, and while I was out there my father, who was Bishop of Lewes, died. I decided I must choose another career which would be safer from a financial point of view than the stage. Oddly enough this strange idea about safety in writing as a career turned out all right in my case." Her first book, a novel for adults, was accepted immediately by publishers in England and America.

Miss Streatfeild has written almost 50 books since that decisive day in Australia. Among her writings for children are the popular "Shoes" books, a series that began with the publication of *Ballet Shoes* in 1936. She has never lost her love for travel, which was developed during her years with the theater. When she was gathering background material for *Circus Shoes*, she spent a summer traveling with the circus. This book, under its British title *The Circus Is Coming* won the Carnegie Gold Medal.

It was not necessary for Miss Streatfeild to travel far to write about the Thames, however. Her London home is very near the river, and she takes frequent walks along the embankment.

*River otter*
Annan Photo Features